© 2010 Galahad Jones

Published by lulu.com

ISBN 978-1-4461-4827-3

To the girl in the bowl
For time and friendship
Love and care always
Galahad

Jealousy

The Fortress

I will shade that radiance
The light behind her eyes
The drapes of my devotion
Will keep her from the skies

Notice me a freedom
I'll launch an insurrection
With savagery and hatred
And tokens of affection

I will be importunate
I will slew and beg
And when she crumbles I'll enfold her
Like a snake across an egg

But the jealousy encrypting
With the fear of being fled
Gives rise to revolution
Now I'm stuck here in the bed

For I have become a fortress
A living breathing shrine
Because I know her real value
And have no idea of mine

Friendship

Aviation

I remember difficult stages
When I needed navigation
And you would stop to help me find the way
Confidently turning pages
Showing me aviation
When all my biggest bridges fell away

You saw me battling regret
And all the trouble it brings
Then whispered to me listen to the wind blow
You can only watch a sunset
Never can you stop things
Just find less painful ways to let them go

We have walked in sunshine
Built history and safe havens
Spoilt each other with care and things for free
On occasion found the line
Kept secrets in all seasons
Right or wrong you're always cool with me

So they tell me on my travels
That you're struggling in vain
As misfortune and your oldest dreams collide
And while utopia unravels
I'll be racing up your lane
Don't go alone in this because of pride

You may have lost this war
So now give up the fight
In life we've known you can't win all your races
But I'll stay near your door
As it would never feel right
For both of us to cry for you in separate places

Corruption

Live and Let Die

Let's keep some secrets
Tell white lies
Pull the wings from butterflies
Betray a lover
Abuse a friend
Break the things we cannot mend

Drink and drive
Scheme connive
Fuel paranoia
Laze and skive mock and jeer
Let jealousy
Interfere

Condition the weak
Watch muscles flex
Preoccupy ourselves with sex

Plunder resources
Reject discourses
Be wasteful with food
Mutilate horses
Impress doctrine generate more
Ignore the slow destroy the poor

Manipulate history
Rape and sack
Befriend a nation break its back
Launch invasions
Take by force
Buy democracy on a golf course

Ethnically cleanse and trade in slaves
Subjugate and dig mass graves
Roll camera smile smarm and vile
Exile despots without trial

Hide technology
Steal shares
Melt the home of Polar Bears
Poison rivers pollute the skies
Pretend that Jesus had blue eyes
Shoot black people kill the sea
Modify biology

Chop down trees put Jews on trains
Smash office blocks with aeroplanes
Develop weapons have crusades
Watch Africa's children die of aids
Put eyes in space control the minions
Split man made atoms and wipe out millions

Romance

Arm in Arm Through Tulips

Arm in arm through tulips
We lay beneath the willow
So softer strokes and gentle grips
Her midriff for my pillow

No gift moreover pleases
Than the tapestry she brings
Stirring perfume breezes
Her books and smiles and things

Geese and swans are soaring
From Maritime to Thames
At peace but lifeblood roaring
In love I know no stems

As a kiss unfurled her care
I promised all my time
The sun chased down the fair
We stood with the Wolfe sublime

We parted hands for slumber
Over dusk beside the Sark
Of all my days when I fell for her
Through the trees in Greenwich park

Denial

Verisimilitude

Your Jones for me has now faded
Your outlook on me is so jaded
But my mind will twist reality
To please me
With confrontation evaded
And all my love paraded
Show congeniality
Appease me

I'll say our love has just begun
Me and you are so much fun
Return your eyes to me
Stay a while
My imploring and it's done
Shrew you see the sun
Hide your apathy
And smile

Paint a picture for me to believe
Convince yourself not to leave
Lay your soft warm skin
On my blues
With my denial in weave
I look on your sleeve
To feign is no sin
Be my muse

Every breath a scream and losing
Only you can fix the bruising
As monsters from the id
Rage over Eden
This is not your choosing
It's all too confusing
So keep it hid
See reason

Rose tint my world though you wilt
This craven lion feels no guilt
As your shadow is pursued
And you're immured
A design you can't jilt
Our world is rebuilt
Verisimilitude
Secured

23

Growing up

Rabbit Face

My little fists covered
By my jumper's woolly sleeves
My little feet kicking
Through the city's autumn leaves
My little heart beating
And my laughter on the breeze
With mater running after
Knowing love gives no reprieve

My little legs running
Through a field chasing rabbits
My little mind learning
Not to pick up naughty habits
My little hands reaching
Though I know I shouldn't have it
With mater running after
Knowing love gives no reprieve

Crashed bike grazed face
Caught red handed in disgrace
Strangers charms ring alarms
City lights and city farms
Riding horses climbing trees
Losing battles losing keys
Can I have some money please

Summer drinks and summer hats
Blocks of ice and blocks of flats
Raising tadpoles in a jar
Getting restless in the car
Steel drums from dustbin lids
Raleigh choppers latch key kids
Mad skills wicked skids

Fragility and growing pains
Throwing stones at passing trains
Croquet hoops and cricket bats
Dr Seuss' funny cats
Holidays and late nights
Tetanus jabs and dog bites
Scruffy streets and scruffy fights

Awkward phases grown up phrases
Fun and games and picking daisies
Absent Pater in the park
Kicking pushbikes after dark
It's madness to conceive
Fantastic to believe
That Mater ran so much
Knowing love gives no reprieve

Loneliness

Vacant Places

Once again the world turns
In to the view of the sun
Its constant rage broken
Only by the peace of sleep
Once again my world yearns
For my discovery of the one
With love so softly spoken
And affection I could reap

The city has made me prey
I can't embrace the rush
I feel too much polarity
To join the competition
The city has seen me decay
I'll never have the crush
Of comfort in familiarity
And joy in repetition

All desires fade to grey
Shadows replacing dreams
Among your million faces
Is it you that I could trust
All desires for me to stay
Amid the siren screams
Die like brake light traces
Aspirations turn to dust

My body is a white room
Everything seems diffused
Partitioned and in despair
All of you treat me starkly
My body is a soul's tomb
Disregarded and confused
People swarm and I stare
Alone through a glass darkly

Away is where I belong
I'm on the clearest path
My photographs displayed
Making perfect as I yawn
Away with my favourite song
Scented candles in the bath
Submerge this razor blade
Vacant places peaceful dawn

31

The Creation of Life

Between the Equinox

Vessels fill and petals stretch
Beneath a runaway sky
The depth of love in Venus
A speck in nature's eye

Reciprocally relentless
Devoted to the core
Rays and rain intertwine
Life ruptures from the floor

Finches fill the tables
Sunlight rules the hours
The sultry my distraction
From all the pretty flowers

Their cotton skirts do swish
Their creamy skin it glistens
Flush my desirous heart
Expose all my ambitions

What lies between the equinox
The design of generation
Wild life and harmony
Encouraging temptation

Further down the day
I wish time were standing still
In perpetual attraction
With eternity to kill

War

Ribbons and Steel

Looking through small windows
Only our faces remain the same
Who knows where the time goes
Or how to measure every frame
With sentimental trinkets
And a two tone photograph
Her grey for auburn ringlets
And days at the cenotaph
So short this brief encounter
Where only loyalty stays pristine
I love her now as I did then
When we were seventeen

I hear him quietly asking
Why does granddad sit in silence
In the British sun we're basking
But I can't escape the violence
I taught him skimming stones
On Lomond's peaceful banks
I shot flesh away from bones
I laid mines for Rommel's tanks
We play card games after dinner
Sometimes I drive him to the beach
I killed so many people
Peace is out of reach

Like clouds the years all blend
These great eras come and go
Scars may fade but we don't mend
Inside we pray you never know
I saw my brothers perish
In a burning armoured car
Only honour left to cherish
And a rat's eighth army bar
Through the milieu slowly
Echo valour where we stand
Ribbons and steel in Whitehall
For the friends we lost in sand

Lust

Slaked in Velvet

Here at last
The moor is cast
Let cross chastise
These butterflies
Run your hands
Around my arms
Run your charms
Around my bed
Throw back your head
Throw back this quilt
Take off these clothes
Take of this guilt
First the fashion
Then the shape
My tongue my teeth
Across your nape
Turn around
And press against me
Rip me break me
Liberate me
Tear away at all my seams
Realise my veiled dreams
Seduce me through
Your every curve
I love your skin
I love your verve
I've got the nerve
To slip and tip
To deepen this relationship
Every sinew fills with tension
Exorcise all my Abstention
The banks give way
And axis broken
I raise my head
And then our eyes met
Filled with passion and
Slaked in velvet

Watch my wrist across my chin
Let the end of this begin
Draw my breath
Along your skin
Pull me in
Anticipation
Hasten spin
Roll and slide
Smile at me
Enjoy the ride
Get wild with me
Self absolved
And full of will
Take the helm
And get your fill
The clash of lips
The frantic grips
Arc your back
And raise your hips
Hold tight your hands
Across my shoulders
Waves and wakes
Becoming bolder
If there could be acceleration
Within so much Intoxication
They'll be no peace
We will not cease
All at once we release
Profiled half light
Glistening lace
Forever hold this state of grace
Collapse
Drop sail
Relax
Exhale

Love

Crop Failure

On a windswept Devon bay
Running across the sand
I caught you laughing in a picture
With an ice cream in your hand

Where so many seeds were sown
As we went walking in the rain
In Woodland down from Lynton
And up Clovellys' cobbled lane

Picking up colourful stones
On the early morning shore
Spending time with shire horses
And watching falcons soar

Through the butterfly houses
And between the fields of gold
Around the wildlife parks
In the greatest romance told

Roaming Salisbury plain
Beneath an autumn sky
We had yet to hear the sound
That doves make when they cry

Now we wage a civil war
Our resentments fill each day
Detractions and defences
Are sending love into decay

Concessions never surface
Without the will to empathise
And truth is fucking jack-knifed
In a labyrinth of lies

As I turn my head away
And my palm toward the floor
The sound of you once cherished
Is slammed behind the door

I'd give up and shoulder blame
Find the strength to walk away
But these children I love so dearly
Will always make me stay

Instead I tear your confidence
And you scar my self esteem
Is there room to let the hatred heal
Or have we really killed a dream

In this horrid spiteful darkness
How are we supposed to grow
Reaping life from one another
And forgetting how to sow

Patriotism

My Flag My Country

Take your place in the arena
Bring your flags and expectations
Draw in the deepest breath
And scream your country's name
As they coil deep in the blocks
Recite your inspirations
If we run away with gold
Things will never be the same

The years hang on a moment
Every nerve absorbs the chalk
So raise your head toward us
As you poise and take the strain
Make the battlefield your own
Blaze a trail where others walk
For half the grit you've shown us
I would swallow all your pain

With my glory in your slipstream
And your steel in every stroke
Should the dream cascade away
In returning show no shame
I will still defend you
Though now you may broke
We'll go stronger higher faster
When they next ignite the flame

But when the rivalry is over
Share your joys and consolations
Pay respects before you leave
For without love there is no game
Now take your place in the arena
Bring your flags and expectations
Draw in the deepest breath
And scream your country's name

The Violation of Children

Forever Neverland

The dream the dream
The naive dream
That divine lightening could intervene
The balance restored
The loved and adored
Once more within the fold

To quietly reminisce
The absent bliss
The secret sleeping bedtime kiss
To cry some more
To try for the door
That will lead to everything

Where you would ride
Or run and hide
The softest glow when you confide
Alone in the dark
Lost in the park
Replaying memories of buried treasure

Shoes to replace
Sports day race
Open arms and choochy face
Snatched from a field and found in another
Pity the mind that has to discover
That the light of the world is gone

That smile beaming
That loving feeling
Do you think it was quiet or was there screaming
An empty womb
In an empty room
Why can't we see your still wheels turning

The print of a hand
A life once planned
Forever to remain in Neverland
We cannot make right
We can only fight
I would pull the trigger and walk away

Humour

The story of Eleanor Greenwood and some stuff that must be true

Eleanor Greenwood
Could not swim
She could not read for she was dim
She had a paraplegic cat
Some furniture from Habitat
A purple scarf and matching hat
She stole from a sleeping pikey
In the factory
She packed boxes
Spat in bags of minty foxes
Another tabard hairnet flunky
Dreams of millionaires all hunky
Of eating eggs laid by a monkey
In posh restaurants for the dim
She was also very slim
Advantages were taken
She had a fading memory of something rude with bacon
She believed in outer space
In things she couldn't spell or taste
That Muppets are the master race
And it's on telly so it's true
She made blue
With an octogenarian
A fat Bavarian and a vegetarian
She fell asleep next to a narcoleptic
Convinced herself her brain was septic
Why are goldfish apoplectic
Then she woke up in Glasgow
Where all the tramps go
To drink and beg
She found a speckled monkey's egg
She scurried home inside a pony
Swallowed it whole with fresh Baloney
Artichokes and mascarpone
In a strawberry marmite sauce
And then of course
She was middle class
Shot her fish and bought a dog
Started yoga kept a blog
Joined a library bloody hell
I think I want to live in Chigwell
Hold on a minute what's that smell
Then she fell over
Supernova
Eleanor Greenwood inside out
Blue tabard red for blood did spout
Passers by saw her explode
The Richter scale the mother load
Intestine covered monkeys were running up the road
I told you it was true

The Abuse of Power

Democracy Inertia

Shroud our true intention
Democracy inertia
Lets us draw our battle plans
For re-arranging Persia

Align ourselves with hawks
Control the thick black rug
Conciliate our family
As it makes them feel snug

We know not veracity
This day would surely come
To see mercenary and nemesis
All rolled into one

Invisible amongst us
Some will carry switches
To take as many as they can
For plundering their riches

Misrepresent the Hansard
Make turbid all the rivers
Be sure to scream inequity
When our enemy delivers

Insecurity

If I Carry You

The sweetest kiss is laced with tension
Love and fear and apprehension
Fragile in all its complication
The chance of me and you
Caught in your corner looking pensive
I fold my arms and get defensive
Deeply cut and introspective
My regrets come in to view

Behind the storm at your window pane
You confide concerns of betrayal again
Afraid you'll feel my friendship wane
And leave you scattered on the floor
You say that love is all disguises
Shams and splits and compromises
But I know that your slow smile rises
When I knock on your door

In your soft room the warmth and flowers
Blend conversation and melt the hours
Rain falls hard between the towers
And shadows draw across your table
I compliment your natural flair
A glance becomes a deeper stare
If you could hold that look right there
In your dress of silken sable

The thunder bellows as we unwind
A kindred scene is hard to find
I think you're stunning and very kind
In flicker and glow you are the one
A big soft chair with our kicked off shoes
Red wine and laughter as candles fuse
And though we know inner city blues
We'll figure out what's going on

Content at last with no disarray
You confess you fell in love today
Whispering as clouds are blown away
To pass me by would be a sin
So if I carry you will you carry me
Can we help each others memory
Adrift as we sway on your balcony
In the moonlight breeze and Marvin

Betrayal and Vengeance

Monsters

From
Chicanery
And duplicity
Insidious betrayal
Unexpected trickery
Demonic hateful bale
All loyalties dissolved
The mystery Revealed
Karma's flow revolved
Showing you concealed
You sacrificed our palace
Deliverance my only value
In your insanity and malice
You said I'd never have you
We engaged in overt cupidity
Like past emperors over Rome
But my arrogance and stupidity
Exposed our secrets in the loam
In cruelty we ruled the darkness
More than princes we were kings
Your violence retained a princess
I pillaged innocent people's things
But invasion came and you sold me
You showed our enemies to the gate
With your cohort you escaped to safety
As I witnessed an empire fall and separate
I have already dug the two graves necessary
Slaughtered all my knaves and retired my emissary
Quartered with slaves and conspired with mercenaries
Tired phased and paranoid unclean dazed and lost in void
All our lives orbit knives blood spattered faces screams and cries
Forfeits paid on lonely drives and scattered traces of dreams and lies
Consumed with vengeance
And drowned in psychosis
These Florentine lessons
Have brought us to this
Like Michael and Fredo
Where else could this go
There is no other scenario
I'll draw in your last breath
As my steel runs you through
After your death they can have me too
Is this a reward that love would allow
This seething terror behind my brow
All is lost
We are monsters now

Passion

Green Hills Through French Windows

I undid the buttons
Down the back of her dress
Gone with the wind
I seduced I confess

Silk evening wear slipped
In the crackle and flame
Rising floods filled my skin
While I whispered her name

The temperature rose
As my kiss became bite
And her grip tore my skin
As the play became fight

From ankle to neckline
One loves to explore
Over curve and through layer
To the soft velvet core

Green hills through French windows
Past cream cotton drapes
La femme remplit le chamber
As the tension escaped

In the warmth of perspire
And the haze of Chanel
The moon began drifting
As the night cast its spell

So straps were retied
And seams were made straight
Slide your shoes back on dear
We are going to be late

Death

Until we meet again

The final day is dawning
I must face this wake
Face this mourning
I know support will come
Arms will open
Tears will flow
I can let my family know
This guilt of feeling numb

Quiet in reflection
Sat face down alone
Looking with affection
Across your small possessions
Your driving licence
The rings you wore
Memories of things you saw
I'll miss all of your expressions

There'll be no school today
The children preparing
Without their fray
Withdrawn in all their sorrow
You'll glide away
They'll set you burning
I'll resent the world for turning
When your not here tomorrow

Flowers lain and blessings made
Speeches heard
Respects are paid
I reveal the depth of grief
Draw my veil quick
And hide my eyes
Keep my anger in disguise
God is a common thief

Waiting patiently left behind
I slow down
With you in mind
Thoughts of you will never wane
I will not surrender
I don't know how
I will honour every vow
Until the day we meet again

The search for contentment

The wood between the worlds

Restless and ill tempered
Ache within the frame
Spyglass in the crow's-nest
Plan another game

From one island to the next
From separation to complete
The theorem that inclusion
Forms ground beneath the feet

Preoccupied with sextants
Mind buried in the charts
Mapping unknown worlds
Perfecting pointless arts

Make reflection to interpret
Or just fill another void
Is it we that need the meadow
Or can I be overjoyed

Unknown to one's own eye
Disappointment could set in
Architect of all the changes
If the changes are within

For all the death in Jadis
The demons will not let it go
Trying to navigate the islands
When it is I that I should know

Slowly come to realise
I can grow so many trees
I can offer fellowship
I have wisdom I have seeds

The wood between the worlds
Lying quietly in the grass
Where I speak so very clearly
Allowing time to gently pass

Religion

And therein lies all the difference

The preacher has spoken
Fields echo the tower
Incense is swung
With the balance of power
The ethos embraced
That death brings reward
Congregations yield faith
Doctrine spread with the sword

In a life of foreboding
A secure sense of place
There is hierarchy and law
Woman cover your face
Enlightened and loved
Compassionate and true
Our beautiful stories
I force upon you

Prayer wheels are spun
As the view becomes sour
Temples are stormed
Roots severed from flower
Now travelled in exile
And resigned to demise
With the spirit diluted
The wisdom dies

In this cycle of conflict
No haven to thrive
As one empire falls
More monsters arrive
Seven million destroyed
To humanity's shame
But hardliners among you
Would consider the same

I hold fast to the centre
And search for perfection
In friendship and movement
Without resurrection
Let these houses of worship
Plan their attack
I know all who have been here
Are not coming back

What was my motivation for writing this collection of poems?

Jealousy
Friendship
Corruption
Romance
Denial
Growing up
Loneliness
The creation of life
War
Lust
Love
Patriotism
The violation of children
Humour
The abuse of power
Insecurity
Betrayal and Vengeance
Passion
Death
The search for contentment
Religion

Where do we fit, what space do we truly, comfortably fill,
amid all of these,
unstoppable things?

Take care of yourself

Galahad Jones.

Acknowledgments

Special thanks to

Karen Brace
Becky Milsom
Steph Hill and NortyJo Davies (keep it ska)
Jackie Wykes was Rose
Andrew Kowalyk
Auntie Ginny
Uncle Jerry
Cliff Kurganshead Schafer
Sam Hardy
Lel Lely Longlegs Butler
Charlie Davies
Mr James B Kirk
Marcus Bro Jones
Miss Sammy Gibbins
Mater
My Sister Sarah Gregory
Sifu James Sinclair
Olusgun Oyekanmi, Respect Brother